Butterfly
Coloring Boook for Adults
Book 2

Sophia Payne

Copyright: Published in the United States by Sophia Payne

Published October 2016

PDF Version this book : http://bit.ly/butterfly_c_2

Don't Miss Another our Books.

http://bit.ly/safari_coloring_b

ISBN : 9781523987931
(Use this ISBN for searching on amazon.com)

www.ingramcontent.com/pod-product-compliance
Lightning Source LLC
Chambersburg PA
CBHW051951280526
45789CB00009B/3253
* 9 7 8 1 5 3 9 9 4 3 8 4 6 *